Of This River

Of This River

POEMS BY **NOAH DAVIS**

WHEELBARROW BOOKS ▪ *East Lansing, Michigan*

⊗ The paper used in this publication meets the minimum requirements
of ANSI/NISO Z39.48-1992 (R 1997) (Permanence of Paper).

Wheelbarrow Books
Michigan State University Press
East Lansing, Michigan 48823-5245

Michigan State University Press
East Lansing, Michigan 48823-5245

Library of Congress Control Number: 2019953143
ISBN 978-1-61186-374-1 (paper)
ISBN 978-1-60917-648-8 (PDF)
ISBN 978-1-62895-409-8 (ePub)
ISBN 978-1-62896-410-3 (Kindle)

Book design by Charlie Sharp, Sharp Des!gns, East Lansing, MI
Cover design by Erin Kirk
Cover art: *Winter 1946* (1946), by Andrew Newell Wyeth, Tempera on board,
31⅜ × 48 in. (79.7 × 121.9 cm), © 2019 Jamie Wyeth / Artists Rights Society
(ARS), New York, used with permission. Holding of North Carolina Museum of
Art, Raleigh, purchased with funds from the State of North Carolina.

green press INITIATIVE Michigan State University Press is a member of the Green Press
Initiative and is committed to developing and encouraging
ecologically responsible publishing practices. For more information about the
Green Press Initiative and the use of recycled paper in book publishing, please
visit *www.greenpressinitiative.org*.

Visit Michigan State University Press at *www.msupress.org*

With the publication of Noah Davis's collection of poems, *Of This River*, the Residential College in the Arts and Humanities (RCAH) Center for Poetry at Michigan State University offers its sixth book in our Wheelbarrow Books Poetry Series. Clearly, we pay homage to William Carlos Williams and his iconic poem, "The Red Wheelbarrow." Readers will remember the poem begins with, "so much depends upon . . ." that red wheelbarrow. As I write this, autumn swirls her colors in the air and punctuates the fields with pumpkins. The butternut squash roll over ready to be plucked from the vines, and the old rusted wheelbarrow rolls through yard and garden collecting the season's beauty. So, we hope, in our books, to collect the treasures of thought and language, the disparate shapes and colors and tastes of the seasons of our lives.

Noah Davis's book is a unique collection of voices that speak from a place where we would often rather not be. But we are, as we read these poems, and the lives lived there are rendered memorable in language brutal, mysterious, and lyrical all at the same time. It's a strange story he tells. "In this valley" things happen. The poems are haunted by the history of the place. There are surprising juxtapositions. A reader might find herself asking, "Is this real? Is this fabricated?" Why do I always feel slightly off-balance?" But there is no doubt that the voice here, behind the multiple voices, is true. Short-Haired Girl, Snapping Turtle, and Coyote, among others, have things to tell us about "the banking sounds of grief's blue / lines which keep us / tethered in this place."

We are at a critical time in the history of our country, and the world, where we need to stand up for the sanctity of the word. Ezra Pound reminds us that "poetry is news that stays news." There is no "fake news" in poetry. We need to understand how language both warps truth and how it defends truth, how poetry utters truths that political speeches and rhetorical flourishes cannot, how poetry evokes in us that which is most human, most universal, and most personal. "What you have heard is true," writes Carolyn Forché as she opens one of the most devastating poems of political brutality written in the last half century, "The Colonel." We may agree with William Butler Yeats, writing in 1919 after the end of WWI:

Things fall apart; the centre cannot hold;
Mere anarchy is loosed upon the world,
The blood-dimmed tide is loosed, and everywhere
The ceremony of innocence is drowned;
The best lack all conviction, while the worst
Are full of passionate intensity.

Poetry helps us understand that we are not alone in our fears and observations by providing a retreat, a place of stillness and contemplation, a place of safety and inspiration. At the end of her chilling political novel, *The Handmaid's Tale*, Margaret Atwood's main character, Offred says, "And so I step up. Into the darkness within; or else the light." Sometimes poetry takes us into the darkness within so that we may, ultimately, step up into the light.

As our number of Wheelbarrow Books increases, we hope that our audience increases also. Help us spread the word. In the beginning was the word, and the word became the poem. So much depends upon the collaboration of reader, writer, and poem, the intimate ways we come to know one another. So much depends upon this relationship.

—ANITA SKEEN, *Wheelbarrow Books Series Editor*

What grabbed me about *Of This River* is its visceral vision. This poet is right next to what he's writing about, be it a grandmother frying snapping turtle to feed her grandkids or a man desperate to father a child slaughtering a bobcat and . . . Well, I'll let you find that out.

What kept me reading was the vividness of the people Noah Davis writes about. *Of This River* brings us a flood of stories, and its central character is Short-Haired Girl, the child engendered by bobcat magic. In elemental ways, she bears the family's hope & its history. Their place—with its buried valley under the reservoir, near the played-out coalfields of Altoona, Pennsylvania—shapes that history in ways that deepen poem by poem.

Finally, the relentless connectedness in *Of This River* wouldn't let me go. The deeper I read into Davis's poems, the clearer it became that everything touches and affects everything else: passion and fear, human and animal, plant and rock, the river running through all creation. Fittingly, the voices in these poems are not human only; we hear from Brown Trout, Mayfly, Snapping Turtle, and even scraps in the compost. For good and ill, nothing exists in isolation.

Mythic, archetypal, down-to-earth, and dirty, *Of This River* is a world unto itself that can make us see our worlds differently.

—GEORGE ELLA LYON

For Home and Family

thank you we are saying and waving
dark though it is.

—W. S. MERWIN

CONTENTS

Of This River

First Memory of Water

Newt coiled round newt
while catfish spawned
and tadpoles,
like oil,
laid between
drowned leaves.

Drowning as Taught by Short-Haired Girl

I don't remember the moment
my head hit the rock because I was still
in the moment of entering water.

But while the water entered me I did
recognize the sleeve of reservoir,
like a fish finning toward the empty

space between my gums and lips.
And as blood billowed from my head,
I thought of the snapping turtles at the base

of the dam, how they waited
in the cold mud for me
to become meat,

a lesson they learned
from eating all those
who drowned before.

Small Histories

At the bridge above the town
boys dare each other to dive
into the green water and swim
inside the fossil of a refrigerator
dumped in this river so long ago
stone has grown around
the open door. Carp shadows quiver
the white metal while boys try
to judge light and current's path.
They bring rocks flecked with mica,
rusted railroad spikes, elk antlers, offerings
with weight to take the boys down
to where they can swim below the river's
flow and exchange their gifts with those
boys before them have left: the teeth
of so many dogs, a bag of brass
rifle shells, a crow's wing
wrapped in bike-chain
and tied to a horse's jaw.

4

Woman Who Will Be Short-Haired Girl's Mother
Plants Potatoes after a Night Trying to Conceive

We were on our knees
      for so many hours I couldn't tell

            the difference between the sweat
            I brought from the garden into bed
            and the sweat I made there.

I sweat into the dirt as I plant the seed potatoes,

each root the size of the fist
I want open and clasping the side
of my breast while she latches.

There is still snow
      where the shadow of the house is longest.

I want to give birth when there is no snow in that shadow.

Want her to live months without cold.
Want her to be able to crawl away from cold
      to where I wash the potatoes
         planted a year before she is pulled from me

and to learn my hands as the smell of the dirt

      she's swallowed in the garden.

Short-haired girl

swims in the old water
running behind the potato patch

while her two mules sleep
so honestly

their cheeks press saucers of heat
into the grass

Corpuscular

Two water thrushes followed me into sleep

and we moved about each other there,

      never touching,

but moving with the intent of touch,

a measured distance I believed I'd always share with birds

even though my grandfather caught goldfinches

and brought them to the cage of his ear

      where they waited

to swallow the banking sounds of grief's blue

lines which keep us

      tethered in this place.

Ridge and Valley as Taught by Short-Haired Girl

Da-Xia's family lives above their restaurant
on 8th street. She asked if the animals
could see me when I didn't wear camo
after I gave her one of my hair ties.

She said that her momma's heart was weak,
and I imagined deer stumbling on talus.
I told Poppa the family would pay forty dollars
for the bear's gallbladder. How the momma's rhythm
could be righted by tea the same color as the salve
Pap makes from black cohosh and rubs
into his swollen knuckles.

The sun opens the forest as Poppa shoots
the black bear in the stream. The animal's
front legs buckle with waves the bullet sends
across the body, and the bear plunges into the pool
below, snout snapping on stone. His bones clicking
as the head bounces on frosted ground
while we drag him with ropes to the truck.

The carcass hangs nose down from a skinning gambrel
in the garage, and blood drips into a bucket where flies drown.
When Poppa strips off the hide, I can see how the bear's shoulder
becomes bicep, and how the elbow bends like mine.

Pap waits with a plastic Sheetz bag as I stretch
stomach muscle, hole opening like a gate. The young
tomato-sized bladder hangs from its vine of liver
and Poppa reaches into the dark.

As we brake at every stop sign,
my thighs flex against the shifting sack,
and my body leeches warmth from the bladder,
until I fear I've sucked away what Da-Xia
and her parents need. What they believe
this bear can give.

Skins

In this valley, where mules catch pigeons
in their mouths, women wrap rattlesnake skins
around their daughter's thighs while babies
wail out from their red rooms.

  Come wailing out and away
from these snake skins with the fear strongest
when we can only see shapes.

  And the fear lives
in these shapes until one day in January
these babies, who have grown into children carrying
their own fear, hike to a talus slope and with axes
chop away a chestnut stump,

  where they find thirty rattlesnakes
curled in cold and kill every one of them.

  These babies, grown large enough
to carry dead snakes in their hands, lay the snakes on the snow
in shapes only hawks can read.

In this valley, where bees build honeycomb
between railroad ties, women wrap rattlesnake skins
around their daughter's thighs while babies
wail out from their red rooms.

When the babies are teething,
these mothers lay rattlesnake skins
on swollen gums.

These babies grow into children
who know what it means to have rattlesnake skins
in their mouths, which they remember as they hike through groves of
bear oak

11

and hear the snake's metallic buzzing
and speak to the snake in a way only bodies who have been together
since breath began know how.

In this valley, where bears walk upright
on the road, women wrap rattlesnake skins
around their daughter's thighs while babies
wail out from their red rooms.

        The mothers wipe mucus and blood
from their babies' cheeks and bellies
with the rattlesnake skins and because the skins

        of these babies are new
the scales mark their cheeks and bellies
until fathers come and scrub away the divoted prints.

        When these babies grow
into girls and boys who want hands to touch them,
they recognize who else was born in this valley

        by rubbing their hands over cheeks
and bellies and finding the keratin-memory of rattlesnake scales
left by mothers.

Learning to Talk to Animals as Told by Short-Haired Girl

I'm skinny and won't show my front
       teeth if I don't have to. But today,
after I broke the stalk of a touch-me-not,
       just how Witch James showed me, I swallowed
the plant's balm and talked for the first time
       to a deer by the river. Our speaking made me
love my tongue more than any sun-warm tomato,
       more than any ground-cold carrot.
The doe told me she hid her fawn
       by a hobble bush, and I said I wouldn't go
look. But while she walked into the field
       to eat, I snuck and found the child
sleeping. I went back to the river
       before the doe crossed again.
I'll hold this lie close, like the teeth
              in my head.

Saint Francis

A Marlboro pinched between his lips, he strains against the weight of a still-warm deer on the road to Fostoria. He uses a rope to raise the dead, a noose around the neck. It's a doe, and she joins the four others in the bed, laying her head on the white belly of the one missing her front legs. He says a prayer as he massages his forearms, muscle bound with a morning's work. At the deer dump, maintained by the Department of Transportation, he rolls the bodies in with hundreds of others. Many rejoice at his return: eagles, vultures, crows, and hawks of nearly every stripe, and the carrion beetles and maggots that offer the benediction by scouring the bones. When he hunts, he loves to warm his hands in the chest of a deer taken in snow. As he grips the steering wheel, he remembers dragging animals by their ankles through fields, leaving behind a bloody language. Before he drives out of the pit, he sounds the truck's horn, and from their perches upon decaying flesh a great menagerie of sated angels beat their wings, leaving behind a sky full of leaden feathers.

Short-Haired Girl Visits Her Cousin Who Moved Back Home Last Week

My cousin told me she was too high to drive and for every gravel bridge
        we'd cross she'd pay me a dollar if I got her to the pizza shop
        and back.

The momma turtle was laying her eggs in the gravel by the road.

My cousin hit me to stop and after she opened her door she fell into the
        gravel.

My cousin threw gravel at the momma turtle laying her eggs.

I honked the horn and my cousin flinched in the gravel, yelled,

If I get gravel in the momma turtle's mouth, the shells'll be hard like gravel,
        and that raccoon will break his teeth, and quit diggin where he
        ought not dig.

Woman Who Catches Kingfishers

Skin broke

              over hemlock boughs,

     while the river swung

                  with the rain of September.

Smoke spun

     through her lips,

          white and blue.

                          Purple

raspberry canes

               ran along her thighs.

     Kingfishers slept where water

        cut the bank.

And ants,

       like bruises,

             moved up her arms.

Short-Haired Girl Goes to Church

The church at the mouth
of the hollow
says
we can cut down
the mountains
because God
will come again
and make them new.

In Sunday school
I ask
what we're supposed to do
when the mountains
are all dust and rubble?

The teacher says
God will provide
for the faithful.

Thursday nights

at the gym
        hands made for
                factory work and
driving trucks
        shoot jump shots.

Wives coin vending machines
        for Mountain Dew and Coke,
babies in carriers propped
along the cinder-block wall receive kisses.

At half-time, if it's not raining,
the refs share a cigarette with
        a point guard
who tells them to watch
        the hip-checks.

Some still believe they can fly
        and take a handful of uppers before
the game: last week one guy dunked
and his finger's still
        caught in the net.

How Blood Becomes the River

Heavy metals settle at the lowest point

                —the bottom of deep tunnels or in the belly

meat of bluegills—flowing with rain

                and thaw, our iron rivers filling the spaces

in the rock we've broken.

Brown Trout Tells Short-Haired Girl about the End of October

Two or three leaves follow

        every caddis that floats overhead.

Through the run, walnuts bob,

        tinting the water sweeter.

These days, the last of the sun

        will reach the stony bottom.

In the next pool

        a deer drifts facedown.

A spike who broke

        his leg crossing.

I glide between antlers,

        cheek hairs sway with the water.

I fin inside his chest,

        golden sides pressing white ribs.

I slide out, wander downstream

        with the rest of the year.

Short-Haired Girl's Brother Watches Her Gut a Deer

Steam lifts around her face
from the deer's open body
like she's lifted the lid
from a pot of beans.

I haven't killed
my first deer yet.
Haven't been inside
any other body
but my own.

I move closer to the warmth.
Her red arms flecked
with white belly hairs
shaved loose by the knife.
She pulls the heart,
lungs, and liver from
the hole she's hacked
in the body.

I ask her
what she feels
when she's elbow
deep. She says
Like us, they're made
of water.

Dream in Which I Sin and Weep Myself Awake

After shooting
a duck, which grew
feathers perfectly,
like trees grew their rings,
I found the crumpled body
under a hawthorn bush
had become a woman
with no torn feathers.
She told me how trees
held fog and rocked
me until I fell away
from her flesh,
like lake weed
sliding off legs
in the shallows.

Kissing the Woman Carried in Bear's Mouth

I move up her side slowly,
examining the scars under her arm and right breast.

I think of the red roots we find each spring after water
takes part of the bank.

> Because I am not bear, I do not chew the hair on the back of
> her head.

I focus on the places bear neglected:
> skin behind the knee,
> mole below the belly button,
> thin muscle between cheek and chin.

But even with this intent,
I roam, and in the dark, find

> like bear found her in the high grass,

two new knots on her collarbone,

tooth-shaped crease on her shoulder,

hesitant rise of ribs struggling to remember

> how much space lungs demand.

Hunger

We will all be ruined when our skin buds

toward whatever body is present, or worse,

when none is present, and we become

the red-tailed hawk on the hay bale waiting

for an updraft to lift us to where we can find

a meal or touch, which is sometimes the same,

the mouth and beak close at the same gait

and hands and talons constrict and relax

on muscle with the same force.

The Language of Silt

The woman whose memory
        sags like heartwood in a dying
alder walks the tangled fence
        line to the creek past the meadow
and calls her sisters' names,
        tongue pressing the backs
of her teeth, hoping she'll find
        some sound lingering in the cracks:
catkin of a word that falls
        and quivers
between pink-rimmed
        toes curled in silt.

Coyote Tells Short-Haired Girl about Loving His Brother

As we slept on the bank
of the long, slow pool,
in light scattered
between willow branches,
I dreamt he hunted
the near field and caught
a rabbit who took his tongue
and carried it into his belly.

I gave him mine, and now
my children trail after his yelp
along the river where I woke
and tried to lick away this story
that crawled from my skull,
through the green milkweed
into his ears.

The Story of the Raven King as Told by Short-Haired Girl's Brother

Two years ago the Raven King learned our faces
when my cousin and I walked the stream.
My cousin called him Raven King, and she

taught him to say his name back to her.
She gave him peanuts or a piece of bread
from a sandwich. Last year the Raven King

spoke our names, called to us as if we belonged
in the stream. In December my cousin brought
the woman who sells okra at the farmer's market

on our walk to meet the Raven King.
On Tuesday I saw my cousin kiss
the woman on a log by the stream. She tilted

toward my cousin like the bubble in a level.
Her hand held my cousin's breast
while the Raven King perched at the end of the log.

Last night in the dark I went to the bottom
of the spruce where the Raven King roosts.
I called his name, shone a light on the oily darkness

of his feathers and shot him. I left him to frost
in the bed of my truck. The Raven King's eye
was sunken like the soft part of a baby's skull.

This morning I brought the Raven King to my cousin,
beak braced shut with dried blood, mud-red
and awkward. We stood on the porch,

the Raven King's body balanced on the rail.
I told my cousin how the first bullet crippled
the Raven King, how bullets three and four

let the air out of his body. Today, I ripped
the Raven King's head away from his neck,
threw it into the garden, and called her pigs,

who I've seen gobble squirrels whole.
My cousin and I watched the pigs
gorge on the Raven King's body.

When the pigs crawled under the porch
to sleep, my cousin left. I laid on the porch
and slept and dreamt I was a rat snake

in the darkness beneath the porch,
swallowing a chipmunk. When I woke
to the stars and no moon, I stumbled

into the garden to find the Raven King's
head between rows of mustard greens.
I pried open the Raven King's beak

with a screwdriver, pulled out his tongue
and searched its pink for the tenderness
the woman gave my cousin.

Murmuration on Bell Tip Road

The boy's skull presses the ceiling as his car
crashes into the truck whose grille sits
next to the engine, glare reaching the space
made by thighs leaving the seat.
Arms shadow the path of wings during flight,
forward around the airbag, then back to complete
the proverb. Teeth drift with the neck
that has moved between headrest and seatbelt.
Glass the width of rain runs across his cheeks,
red prints like the feet of starlings. The single
note the boy believes to be song collides
with his mouth, floods the streambed
of his body and eddies on the pavement.

Lightnin' Hopkins Returns as a Bluetick Hound

The moon's half-light

    shapes water

around a rock

    like the legs

of a woman who left me

    to sleep with her hound

before the ridge of her hamstring

    could be memorized.

Short-Haired Girl's Grandmother Speaks of the Dead

Men killed by trains sit on my porch.

Tonight, the drunk who fell asleep
with his head on the rail rocks beside me.
We watch the nighthawks follow
skippers into the sky.

The conductor who killed the drunk
climbs the steps an hour later.
His chest and face sunken
like a horse's print in mud
from where the freight engine
carried him up the mountain.

He tells us his child is sick,
but cool nights will help the fever.

His wife stares past him and sleeps
on the far edge of the bed,
blankets curled tight around her legs.

I don't speak.
Don't let any of them
know they're dead.

What Names the Moon Gives

Blood beneath my fingernails swells
purple like wild grapes during the third week
of October when men smoke by the river
and wait for the current to rise.
Trains from Pittsburgh scream
from the banks, and cousins who sleep
alone in fear of the space winter brings
turn over to face empty walls. Walking
the mountain's spine to where the trees break,
I remember the way my brother collected
black walnuts, his shirt soaked with millrace,
skin of his hands burnt green.
The day my grandfather died
my brother and I laid in the twin beds upstairs
and fell asleep while our father dropped
into the open cavern of his father's mouth,
resting on his tongue. When I was a child,
a woman held my hand after church
and told me our souls become color
and fall like the moon in the high water
of early April.

Short-Haired Girl's Aunt Tells Her about November Again

Fourteen bears were in the neighbor's corn.

When I walked the tree line on the eastern side of the field I thought the
broken stalks looked like broken legs.

I saw fourteen dark shapes cross the road in the evening. No cubs.
Fourteen full-grown bears entering the cornfield. Rupturing
the cornfield. Splintering the rows. Flaying the ears.

I stood on my stoop wearing my purple robe and ate the last two
peaches of the year. Straining to hear the bears in the brown
field. When trucks drove by I waved, hoping a bear would step
out of the cornfield and the driver would be waving at me and
hit the bear.

Your cousin was hit by a train. Your cousin and her boyfriend were high
and naked and lying on the tracks and hit by a train.

I want to see how other animals open when they're hit.

There were no deer in the corn.

No deer wanted to be near fourteen bears.

No deer, only blackbirds.

So many blackbirds in the corn because the bears stripped cobs with
their teeth, leaving behind kernels in the mud. Three-hundred
blackbirds flew from the field when I walked there. Blackbirds
are fine with bears in the corn. I saw blackbird prints on bear
prints.

I saw your cousin's body on the boy's body. Milled together. Shattered
together.

Fourteen bears in the corn.

No deer.

Only blackbirds.

In fields where junco

wings strike goldenrod stalks

      in the dark
            my future child visits

her mouth opens and closes

      while two basswood trees

      on the hill mark
            each other's trunks

wind swirls clockwise

      through their crowns

I say *widow maker*

            and she

not before morning

      so we wait together

      until the limbs long ago

broken and caught dead

      in the canopy

         fall to earth

where storms
         also collapse

What Was Left

After men cut trees to dirt and stone,
coal was drawn up tunnels and cast
into light like rat snakes from winter dens
or the coiled intestines hands pull
from slaughtered pigs.

Short-Haired Girl Praises a Child on a Horse

When I see a child sitting on a horse, I believe
for a moment they are the same animal.

Like owls sleeping in larch trees.
Like geese resting between cattails.

I believe this more if the child
isn't wearing a shirt.

Like hummingbirds sipping cardinal flowers.
Like dragonflies drying wings on laurel.

If they cross a river, the child and horse
become even closer, a single wet body.

Like bees trembling spicebush.
Like lacewings climbing moss.

Out of the river, water drips down
the child's legs and over the horse's stomach.

River water becomes child's water.
Child's water becomes horse's water.

Water must return to earth.
Like all children and their horses.

Mending

Something there is that doesn't love a wall,
That wants it down.
—Robert Frost

When I lie down with your
back against my chest, I think of how
my grandfather stacked river stone,
one upon another, building a wall
along the edge of the meadow.
And as my palm holds your hip,
I imagine the ball of bone
beneath the flesh, resting
like the cat at the foot of the bed.
And just as my grandfather would walk
the walls in April to find where
stones had cracked and crumbled,
I meander your body, placing my lips
on the backs of your legs, the bend
in your back, your neck that strains
under the day's labor. And where lips
cannot reach, words act like the oval
rocks we wedged into crevices,
saving the wall that keeps
the world from our bed.

38

Short-Haired Girl's Aunt Tells Her about the Woman Who Eats the River

The summer before last
the woman gave your uncle
a glass filled with a late-August
riffle, a kiss thick with tricos
and rising trout.

Some nights I find him
on the back porch,
looking toward the river,
watching the chimney swifts
disappear, a whisper of mayflies
on his lips.

Feeding Hogs as Taught by Short-Haired Girl

I'm not sloppy when I slop the hogs.

I sneak cornbread under my shirt when Momma's not looking.

I throw it to them after they're done with the browned rinds.

I'll taste this June cornbread in March when Poppa fries bacon.

It all hollers back, like everything on this side of the mountain.

That's why everything tastes like the water.

Every day is a god

After Annie Dillard

The change in the sun's

       strength on bittercress

after the first of April

       and the way pear tendrils

catch between teeth

       while the rest of the fruit rubs

the back of the throat in October

       are two joys separated by seasons

bound across months by light

       sugared with sap and northern flickers

who drill the sweet and whose song

       sends us tumbling mouth first

so we have no choice but to taste what is firm.

Oil as Taught by Short-Haired Girl

Gram kept snapping turtles in used oil drums by the garage. Barrels full
of spring water. Not oil. We fed the turtles watermelon until shit covered
the water's surface. My brother and I skimmed off the flakes like oil.
When Gram was ready, we turned the barrels over in the yard, and she
shot the turtles in the head with the .22 Pap gave her. He believed you
gave guns to the people you loved. She used a hatchet to break the shells.
The shards in the grass were sharp and cut our feet. The meat boiled in
vinegar for an hour on the stove. My brother and I watched Gram blow
held-breaths of cigarette out the window. She stared at the pumpjack
in the back field that brought oil to the surface from beneath the sheep.
Gram's thumbnail was orange from tar and my brother asked why it
wasn't black. That's why turtle meat was pink, because watermelon meat
was pink. Gram laughed and said if we peeled her far enough she'd
be dark as oil. My brother dipped the meat into the yellow egg wash,
and I forked together flour, cornmeal, cayenne. Gram heated lard that
turned to oil, the pink meat disappearing into its bubbles. We waited
for the meat to float to the surface so we could pick out what looked
like golden tongues with tongs. Gram dabbed a piece on a paper towel.
She kept an ashtray by the sink, and with her left hand stubbed out her
cigarette while she held out the meat. My lips curled back from the heat,
and I tore the muscle away with my teeth. How much oil in me? How
much oil in her? Someday, when we both became the ground, would a
pumpjack find the oil our bodies left in the clay?

Winter Solstice

After squalls fill the hollow

      I fear the light,
             which has nearly folded
             its purple into laurel,

will splinter on a porcupine's orange teeth
      as it rakes the white ribs of a dead coyote,

vibration sending the tiny bones
      in my inner ear to search for less brittle

sound in the horns of water
      ice curls behind mid-stream rocks

43

or the places where deer

melt snow to the oval shape
of their heat.

Short-Haired Girl's Dead Cousin Visits

Let me unzip my shadow
and hook it to yours.
When the light shifts
you'll feel me tug
the bottoms of your feet
and you'll remember me:
waiting in a hollow
with all the birds
I ever killed,
like we waited
for July heat
to leave the train tracks
in the evening.

I never told you
about slitting
the moon's yolk
and how it smelled
the same as our valley
before Pap
and his poppa
shaved the mountains
bare as sheep nipples.

Can you still smell me?
Is it the same as before
my splitting?

June Evening

We lie on the ground and I run my thumbs
along the ravine your calf muscle and shin build.

Because you haven't shaved in four days
I think I can feel your hair still growing up

between the grooves of my skin,
like the lightning bugs crawling

up from the dirt in our yard.

Short-Haired Girl's Father Catalogues Summer Afternoon

My son waits for river water to dry between his toes

      while he watches writing spiders trace swallows
         across blades of grass.

The cow, in the barn's shadow, blinks away bluebottle

      flies with eye lashes long enough that if my daughter stands
         close, she can feel the air on her chin.

My wife hoes rows of potatoes,
         blossoms soft and veined like tree frog bellies.

I count the green places on the mountain where the trees are new.
         Thankful they're too young to cut.

First Love as Told by Short-Haired Girl

The sun-burnt boy fed me nettles
by the pool where I'd seen him stumble
over stones to catch crayfish. He folded
the leaf so the biting hairs wouldn't
touch my lips, the insides of my mouth,
the back of my throat. I took the leaf
from his fingers, told him I was scared
of the burning. *I creased it tight*, he said,
like a letter. His fingers were bruised
from rocks—*Just rocks*, he said—
and I wanted to touch them with mine.
What did it mean for someone so young
to have swollen fingers? Would he be more
gentle? Would he pull away even before it hurt?

Map of the Body

What we eat was left by fire and the sea.
Trout trapped in steep ridges that used
to be reefs. Blackberry canes spiral from
ash, and long, red hair hides the skin
on your back, white like the skulls
of drowned animals we find at the bottom
of streams. Birds know more about God
the closer they fly to the sun. Let carp
eat the dead. I'll stand naked in a field
where grass sways beneath the moon,
praying you'll trace your fingers over
what shadows mark the edges of my body.

Short-Haired Girl Dreams of Her Family

Momma picked
raspberries in July,
fingers purple like kidneys.

When Poppa dug
postholes, the fire
that hid inside
the clay climbed
the trunks of his legs.

My brother fought with his
teeth, the rage of railroad
tracks and cheekbones.

Menstruation as Taught by Short-Haired Girl

Gram said the first time she spilt herself,

> a buck smelled her blood
> and came to her while she worked
> in the field.

I'd never thought about coupling
with a deer, and I don't think
he'd ever thought of a woman
in that way.

When I spilt myself,
        no deer,
        or fox,
        or bear

                came to my smell
                        even though I bled for days.

I buried every rag I soaked through.

Momma found me
burying them
in the field
                and asked how long I'd been spilling.

I told her

that a boy or baby wouldn't cling to me,
love the smell of me enough
                to hold to my insides.

No deer came to me,

she said while we walked in the field toward home.

Your father did, but he's no deer.

Lottery Tickets

The trailer sits on cinder blocks by the river. An air conditioning unit coughs in the bedroom where a little girl naps and dreams of huckleberries. The red truck outside is brown with rust, and where water flows from a pipe at the paper mill, fish swim sideways, tumors on their cheeks and zinc coating their gills. A man sits in the pick-up and eats the fried bits of silver fish he caught in the river, a dollar bill in his pocket listens to the ball growing in his stomach, white and ridged. After driving the gravel road to the convenience store, he asks the woman behind the register for a pack of Pall Malls, then turns and pushes a dollar into the lottery machine. Inside the electric box, the bill falls next to fives, tens, twenties, crinkled and torn. Some smell of alcohol, or perfume, while his is blotched with the blood of a deer he shot in a farmer's field at night. He remembers the animal green eyes transfixed by the truck's high beams, brown velvet body unable to move as the bolt slid the bullet into the chamber, flash of gunpowder sparking orange and yellow and black.

Short-Haired Girl Visits Her Brother

I had water in my body
where water had never been.
But my body found it familiar.
I think the hog was familiar with this.
I think those turned apples we fed him
before Poppa knelt before him with the rifle
was a taste that made the moment familiar.
Pap said the fire we used to boil the water
that scalded the skin so we could scrape
off the hog's hair was of the fire that burned
off the mountain side and left blueberries
where blueberries had never been.
I am full of water like the blueberries.
I feel raked smooth like the hog.

August Market

Mennonites sell tomatoes and oatmeal cookies
in the dirt pull-off beside the river that bows
back into the mountain. Flies land on pies,
and the red of cherries sticks to the underside
of plastic wrap. The man with glasses
and a walking stick sits on the guardrail
on the other side of the parking lot until
an eighteen-wheeler from Nebraska parks
and he crawls in with the driver for twenty minutes.
A Mennonite woman drops peaches into a green bag
and wipes sweat from beneath her chin,
dark ivy of hair curling behind the ear.
Girls fill cartons with green beans and whisper
under the tent about the ridges of muscle
growing on the boys who helped build the shed
next to the sawmill. Slumping out of the cab, the man
dabs blood from a burst lower lip, blue handkerchief
turning purple. He stares across the road as the truck
lurches through browning thistle onto asphalt.
The man nods at the girls, hears the hollow thump
of a ripe watermelon struck by a finger.

Snapping Turtle Tells Short-Haired Girl about Loneliness

Our beaks made the muted sound
of rocks colliding underwater.
She would wake when trout
began to rise, rub her ivory
underbelly against my leathered neck
as we rolled through the shallows
and into the riffle above the pool
where cows would stand
on hot June days until fireflies
called out against the black
in the hope someone
would answer.

What It Means for the Bear to Eat Ash

Three brothers drive to the mountains
the first warm day of the year
in search of bears asleep, last meat
holding in caves water carved
before the water left.

Menthols and Skoal, fries and beer
leak through the lines of the hands
colored with coal, black as winter
rivers, breath like fur untouched
by light for months.

Oil from the rifle barrel tattoos the green
leaves of rhododendron, a prayer
for the blood-trail they hope to paint.

The last sunny day of September, the youngest
stepped on a broken bottle with bare feet, white
skin flowing around the boulder of his heel.
He walks with a limp behind his siblings,
four-month-old scar screaming beneath the sock.

At the blueberry field, the brothers start a fire
from winterkilled trees and fry bacon
for sandwiches. In August the middle boy
hunted rattlesnakes with cane and bucket,
his father paying five dollars a rattle.

The oldest brother waits for news
from Norfolk Southern before deciding
whether to enlist. For the past five nights,
he's dreamed of walking the bottom

of the reservoir, finding the short-haired girl
who drowned last June, holding her in his arms,
the two of them floating like dogwood petals
over the spillway.

⌒

Bombarded by the songs of tufted titmice,
a bear crawls from his den. Fuzzy eyed,
he makes his way to a seep under a grove
of hemlocks where the ground flows and bends.
Neck thin and frayed as a grapevine, he drinks
away the taste of acorns and smells burnt pig fat.
Finding the ring of stones, he sends his tongue
into the fire's corpse, ash floating up, covering
his face, a mask as delicate as spider webbing.

The oldest brother glasses the bear, motions
for the middle boy to click off the safety,
while the youngest stares into the bottom
of the fold where railroad tracks cross
the river's cheek. When the middle brother
takes the shot, sunlight glints off the scope,
the oldest already running the ridge.

The bear comes to rest in a patch
of crushed raspberry canes. The youngest
slides down the talus slope, calling
to his brothers. The thorns spinning
from the animal's skull are the color
of the dresses their mother used to wear.

February New Moon

After fitting rags into the cracks
around the door with a butter knife,

I sit on the couch next to you and begin
the story of following the bobcat's tracks

to where he fell through the river's ice.
But you kiss me with your tea-warm

mouth before I can draw the blue
outline of the hole with my finger

on your wrist. I keep my eyes open
as you remind me that we are all taught

certain contours before this life,
even while the moon is young

and has no light to give.

Short-Haired Girl's Father Confesses Her Conception

After my wife and I laid in a turned field with the waxing moon
      watching.

After I boiled nettles and served them with cornbread.

After I made her bloodroot tea sweetened with red clover, I knew I was
      too weak to reach where flesh is spun.

I visited Witch James where Bucks Run swallows Kettle Run.

He crushed the fruit of devil's walking stick, mixed it with birch bark,
      and asked if I could smell milk or dirt.

When I said *well water,* he spat.

I paid him chicken livers and a mule's hoof for the shaved ginseng.

It won't make the bobcat's pecker taste better, but it'll help get yours up.

I waited at the bottom of a draw where I'd seen the bobcat cross the
      trickle of a spring.

I didn't like to hunt at night.

When I was a child, Pa said animals didn't have souls. Behind his back,
      Ma shook her head.

I feared that once I unbound the spirit from the body it might have
      trouble seeing in the dark and come barreling into me.

The bullet curled the tom, who in death did not drop the rabbit, and I
      left her in his mouth while I removed his member.

His penis turned over the fire like rotting stinkhorn.

I ate in the woods.

I waited there, as I do after killing, to see if what I'd taken would stay down.

Short-Haired Girl Stops Going to Church

> Samson turned aside to look at the lion's carcass, and in it
> he saw a swarm of bees and some honey. He scooped out
> the honey with his hands and ate as he went along.
> —Judges 14:8-9

My donkey, Dame's Rocket,
found a goat's skull
in the back pasture.

She carried it to me
in her mouth and I nailed
the bone above the door
of her shed. She admired
the skull like I admire antlers.

Bees waxed honeycomb
in the eye sockets, and amber
bulged over the nose where
the lower jaw used to be.

Honey dripped from the skull
onto Dame's Rocket. She licked
the sweet from her muzzle.

The bee's hum settled in the darkest
hair lining her shoulders and I felt
the whirr in my legs when I rode her
around the yard.

Two months ago, I woke before the bees

and sat in front of Dame's Rocket's shed.
I waited there for her to stand below
the bone-hive. Dozens of bee bodies,
barely large enough to catch the light,
slanted around her head,
golden buzzing like the hymns
at church that made me cry.

I stood and reached for the bone-hive
the same way Thomas must've reached
into his savior's ribbed-hive.

The honey was bee-warm
on my fingers and I tasted
the sweetness forever and ever.

Amen

ACKNOWLEDGMENTS

My thanks to the editors of the following journals or publications in which these poems first appeared, sometimes in different form.

Aethlon: "Thursday nights"
Appalachia: "Brown Trout Tells Short-Haired Girl about the End of October" (as "Brown Trout on the Coming of November") and "Coyote Tells Short-Haired Girl about Loving His Brother" (as "Coyote Tells the Story of Loving His Brother")
Atlanta Review: "What Names the Moon Gives"
basalt: "Corpuscular," "Small Histories," and "Oil as Taught by Short-Haired Girl" (as "Oil")
Best New Poets: "Short-Haired Girl's Father Confesses Her Conception"
Blue Collar Review: "How Blood Becomes the River"
Blueline: "Dream in Which I Sin and Weep Myself Awake"
Chautauqua: "Woman Who Catches Kingfishers" and "How Blood Becomes the River"
Cumberland River Review: "What It Means for the Bear to Eat Ash"
Farming: "Feeding the Hogs as Taught by Short-Haired Girl"
Hiram Poetry Review: "Lottery Tickets" (as "The Lottery")
The Hollins Critic: "First Memory of Water"
Natural Bridge: "Saint Francis"
North American Review: "Lightnin' Hopkins Returns as a Bluetick Hound"
Orion: "Short-Haired Girl Praises a Child on a Horse" (as "Other Forms of Water")
Parhelion Literary Magazine: "The Language of Silt"
Permafrost: "Short-Haired Girl's Aunt Tells Her about the Woman Who Eats the River" (as "Woman Who Eats the River")
Pittsburgh Poetry Review: "Short-Haired Girl Dreams of Her Family" (as "Stains")

Poet Lore: "Mending"

Terrain.org: "Short-Haired Girl Goes to Church," "Winter Solstice," "What Was Left" (as "What Was Left of Altoona after I Was Born")

Water~Stone Review: "Snapping Turtle Tells Short-Haired Girl about Loneliness" (as "Snapping Turtle on Loneliness")

"Mending" was nominated for a Pushcart Prize by *Poet Lore*.

"Saint Francis" was nominated for a Pushcart Prize by *Natural Bridge*.

"Lottery" was reprinted in the *Looking at Appalachia* Call and Response Series.

"Oil as Taught by Short-Haired Girl," "Short-Haired Girl Stops Going to Church," "Short-Haired Girl's Dead Cousin Visits," "Short-Haired Girl Praises a Child on a Horse," and "Small Histories" won the 2019 Chapter Career Award from the National Society of Arts and Letters, Bloomington, Indiana Chapter.

Thank you to Lincoln Memorial University for their support through the 2018 Jean Ritchie Fellowship in Appalachian Writing.

Thank you to the Bread Loaf Environmental Writers' Conference and for their support through a Katharine Bakeless Nason Fellowship.

Thank you to the public lands and waters of Pennsylvania.

Thank you to the following people for their love as I make poems: Tanya and Wendell Berry, Dave, Bruce, and Marcia Bonta, Taylor Brorby, James Crews, Christine Cusick, Jim Daniels, Bob DeMott, Chris Dombrowski, David James Duncan, Kurt and Carolyn Engstrom, K. A. Hays, Henry Hughes, Helen Kiklevich, Doug and Sue Miller, Sean Prentiss, Aimee Nezhukumatathil, Jack Ridl, Scott and Ruth Sanders, and Derek Sheffield.

Thank you to my classmates at Indiana University. You make my words better.

Thank you to Cathy Bowman for helping me see where my poems were walking, and giving them a drink.

Thank you to Stacey Lynn Brown for showing me who was trying to speak.

Thank you to Ross Gay for elbows in the chest, telling me to box out, counting twos as ones, and then sitting beneath the basket and talking poems.

Thank you to Adrian Matekja for telling me to write like I'm hungry.

Thank you to Dave Shumate and Michael McGriff for giving extra attention to this manuscript. I hope you see your own effort in these poems.

Thank you to Michigan State University Press. An honor.

Thank you to George Ella Lyon for selecting these poems for the Wheelbarrow Books Poetry Prize, and to Anita Skeen, the director of the Center for Poetry at the Residential College in the Arts and Humanities. You made my dream come true.

Thank you to Mom and Nathan, who remind me that I am writing poems. And for laughing with me. I like it when we laugh.

Thank you to Dad who showed me that I could write poems, taught me how to write poems, helped me with every single poem. I would not be a writer and these poems would not be, if you were not my mentor.

Thank you to my jewelweed, my love, Nikea. We will have blue and purple flowers in our garden.

Thank you to the mountains, rivers, animals, birds, and fish. Never-ending thankfulness.

Praise Be.

Praise.

SERIES ACKNOWLEDGMENTS

We at Wheelbarrow Books have many people to thank without whom *Of This River* would never be in your hands. We begin by thanking all those writers who submitted manuscripts to the sixth Wheelbarrow Books Prize for Poetry. We want to single out the finalists, Sarah Cooper, Dorsey Craft, Laura Goldberg, and Nicole Robinson, whose manuscripts moved and delighted us and which we passed on to the judge, along with Noah Davis's manuscript, for her final selection. That judge, George Ella Lyon, we thank for her thoughtful selection of the winner and her critical comments offered earlier in this book.

Our thanks to Lydia Barron, Grace Carras, Allison Costello, Cindy Hunter Morgan, Amy Potchen, Estee Schlenner, Elizabeth Sauter, and Arzelia Williams for their careful reading of manuscripts and insightful commentary on their selections, and especially to Laurie Hollinger, assistant director at the RCAH Center for Poetry, who also read the manuscripts and provided the logistical aid and financial wizardry for this project. Sarah Teppen, a previous RCAH Center for Poetry intern, designed our Wheelbarrow Books logo, which makes us smile every time we see it.

We go on to thank Stephen Esquith, dean of the Residential College in the Arts and Humanities, who has given his continued support to the RCAH Center for Poetry and Wheelbarrow Books since their inception. As we began thinking seriously about Wheelbarrow Books, conversation with June Youatt, then provost at Michigan State University, was encouraging and MSU Press director Gabriel Dotto and assistant director/editor-in-chief Julie Loehr were eager to support the efforts of poets to reach an eager audience. We cannot thank them enough for having faith in us, and a love of literature, to collaborate on this project.

Thanks to our current Editorial Board, Sarah Bagby, Gabrielle Calvocoressi, Mark Doty, George Ellenbogen, Carolyn Forché, Thomas Lynch, George Ella Lyon, and

Naomi Shihab Nye for believing Wheelbarrow Books a worthy undertaking and lending their support and their time to our success.

Finally, to our patrons: without your belief in the Wheelbarrow Books Poetry Series and your generous financial backing we would still be sitting around the conference table adding up our loose change. You are making it possible for poets who have never had a book of poetry published, something that's becoming harder and harder these days with so many presses discontinuing their publishing of poetry, to find an outlet for their work. You are also supporting the efforts of established poets to continue to reach a large and grateful audience. We name you here with great admiration and appreciation:

Beth Alexander

Mary Hayden

Jean Kruger

Patricia and Robert Miller

Brian Teppen

WHEELBARROW BOOKS

Anita Skeen, *Series Editor*

Sarah Bagby	Carolyn Forché
Mark Doty	Thomas Lynch
George Ellenbogen	Naomi Shihab Nye

Wheelbarrow Books, established in 2016, is an imprint of the RCAH Center for Poetry at Michigan State University, published and distributed by MSU Press. The biannual Wheelbarrow Books Poetry Prize is awarded every year to one emerging poet who has not yet published a first book and to one established poet.

SERIES EDITOR: Anita Skeen, professor in the Residential College in the Arts and Humanities (RCAH) at Michigan State University, founder and past director of the RCAH Center for Poetry, director of the Creative Arts Festival at Ghost Ranch, and director of the Fall Writing Festival

The RCAH Center for Poetry opened in the fall of 2007 to encourage the reading, writing, and discussion of poetry and to create an awareness of the place and power of poetry in our everyday lives. We think about this in a number of ways, including through readings, performances, community outreach, and workshops. We believe that poetry is and should be fun, accessible, and meaningful. We are building a poetry community in the Greater Lansing area and beyond. Our undertaking of the Wheelbarrow Books Poetry Series is one of the gestures we make to aid in connecting good writers and eager readers beyond our regional boundaries. Information about the RCAH Center for Poetry at MSU can be found at http://poetry.rcah.msu.edu and also at https://centerforpoetry.wordpress.com and on Facebook and Twitter (@CenterForPoetry).

The mission of the Residential College in the Arts and Humanities at Michigan State University is to weave together the passion, imagination, humor, and candor of the arts and humanities to promote individual well-being and the common good. Students, faculty, and community partners in the arts and humanities have the power to focus critical attention on the public issues we face and the opportunities we have to resolve them. The arts and humanities not only give us the pleasure of living in the moment but also the wisdom to make sound judgments and good choices.

The mission, then, is to see things as they are, to hear things as others may, to tell these stories as they should be told, and to contribute to the making of a better world. The Residential College in the Arts and Humanities is built on four cornerstones: world history, art and culture, ethics, and engaged learning. Together they define an open-minded public space within which students, faculty, staff, and community partners can explore today's common problems and create shared moral visions of the future. Discover more about the Residential College in the Arts and Humanities at Michigan State at http://rcah.msu.edu.